THE AMAZING BOOK OF

INSECT

RECORDS

THE HEAVIEST, THE LOUDEST, THE MOST POISONOUS, AND MANY MORE!

SCHOLASTIC INC.

New York   Toronto   London   Auckland   Sydney
Mexico City   New Delhi   Hong Kong

Special Thanks
The publisher would like to thank Dr. T.J. Walker, of the University of
Florida, for his help and cooperation in putting this book together.

ISBN 0-439-21722-9

18 17 16 15   10 11 12 13 14/0

Printed in the U.S.A.   40

First Scholastic printing, October 2000

Photo Credits
Cover and title page: © Corel Corporation; pages 4, 8: © PhotoDisc; pages 5-7, 9, 11,
13-15, 19, 27: © Ed S. Ross; pages 10, 12, 16-18, 22, 24-26, 28, 30, 31: © Corel
Corporation; page 20, 21: © J. H. Robinson/Photo Researchers, Inc.; page 23: © LSF
OSF/Animals Animals; page 29: © George K. Bryce/Animals Animals.

Illustrations by Richard MacCabe

Contents

What's the FASTEST insect?

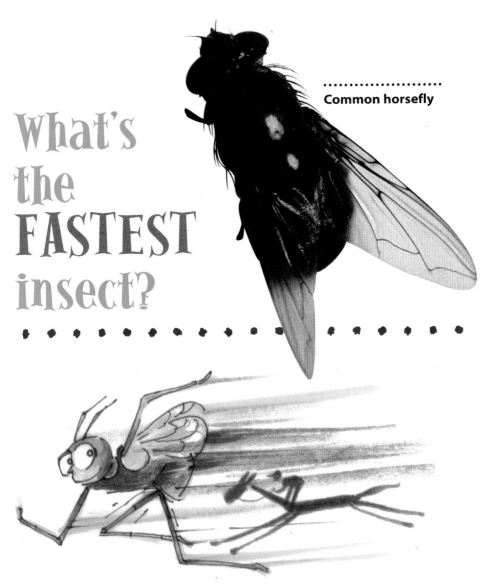

Common horsefly

The Horsefly

This zippy kind of true fly can reach speeds of more than 90 miles per hour (145 kph)!

There are more than 3,500 species of horseflies in the world. In many species, the females suck blood from animals (up to 3 ounces per day). They do this to get protein to develop eggs. Males only feed on nectar and pollen.

This horsefly is biting into human skin.

What's the LONGEST-LIVED insect?

The Wood-Boring Beetle

Certain species of this beetle can remain in a larva stage for more than 50 years!

Wood-boring
beetle (adult)

Wood-boring beetle (larva)

What's the insect with the DEADLIEST POISON?

The Harvester Ant

Ounce for ounce, these ants have the most toxic venom of any insect. Only 12 harvester ant stings are needed to kill a 4.4 pound (2 kilogram) rat!

These harvester ants are building a nest in the Arizona desert.

What's the LOUDEST insect?

The African Cicada

This cicada produces a calling song that has been recorded at 106.7 decibels at a distance of about 20 inches (50 centimeters). As a comparison, a jackhammer operates at about 100 decibels! (Anything over 85 decibels can be dangerous for the human ear.)

Cicada

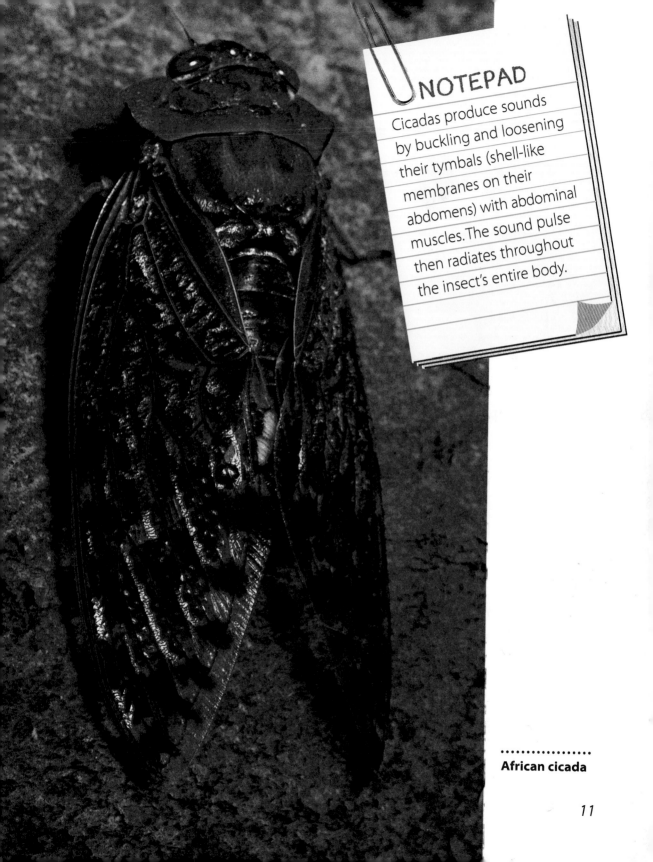

African cicada

What's the HEAVIEST insect?

The Goliath Beetle

This behemoth beetle can weigh up to 4 ounces (100 grams), which is the weight of a quarter-pounder hamburger!

Atlas beetles are some of the largest beetles.

A male and female
Goliath beetle cling
to an adult man's arm.

NOTEPAD

Goliath beetles are not only heavy, they're also big. Some can grow up to 4.5 inches (100mm) in length. A Goliath beetle is so strong that it can actually peel a banana with its forelegs!

What's the SMALLEST insect?

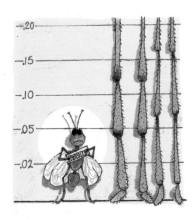

The Parasitic Wasp

One species of parasitic wasp has been recorded as the smallest overall adult insect, measuring only .05 inches (.139 centimeters). That's only a little larger than the smallest segment shown on a ruler!

....
Tiny brachnoid parasitic wasp

NOTEPAD

These tiny wasps use their stingers to deposit their eggs inside the bodies or eggs of other insects. As the larvae grow, they feed on and eventually kill their host.

An adult parasitic wasp walks along the body of a caterpillar that has been host to many cocoons.

What's the LONGEST insect?

The Stick Insect

The longest stick insect ever officially measured was nearly 22 inches (55.8 centimeters) long! That's the length of two sheets of copy paper set end-to-end!

Some stick insects have wings.

This species of stick insect is one of the longest in Asia.

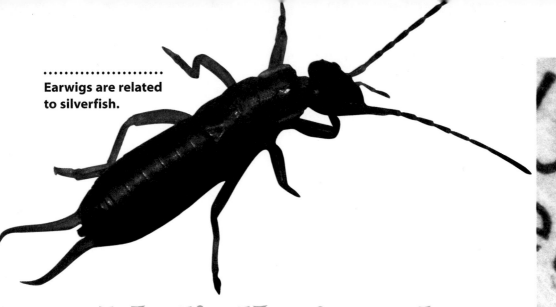

Earwigs are related to silverfish.

What's the insect with the MOST MOLTS?

The Fire Brat (also called Silverfish)

When an insect molts, it sheds its outer shell to make room for a new, larger one. Certain insects undergo many molts as they mature from larvae (developing insects) to adults. The fire brat seems to be the all-time record-holder for molts: it molts 60 times before reaching adulthood.

Common silverfish

NOTEPAD

Some fire brats can live for up to a year without food. They prefer warm temperatures and can commonly be found under rocks and bark, or in basements. They are also particularly fond of eating the glue in books!

19

Carpenter ant queen

What's the insect that lives the LONGEST ADULT LIFE?

The Queen Ant

Certain queen ants have lived to be nearly 30 years old in the wild!

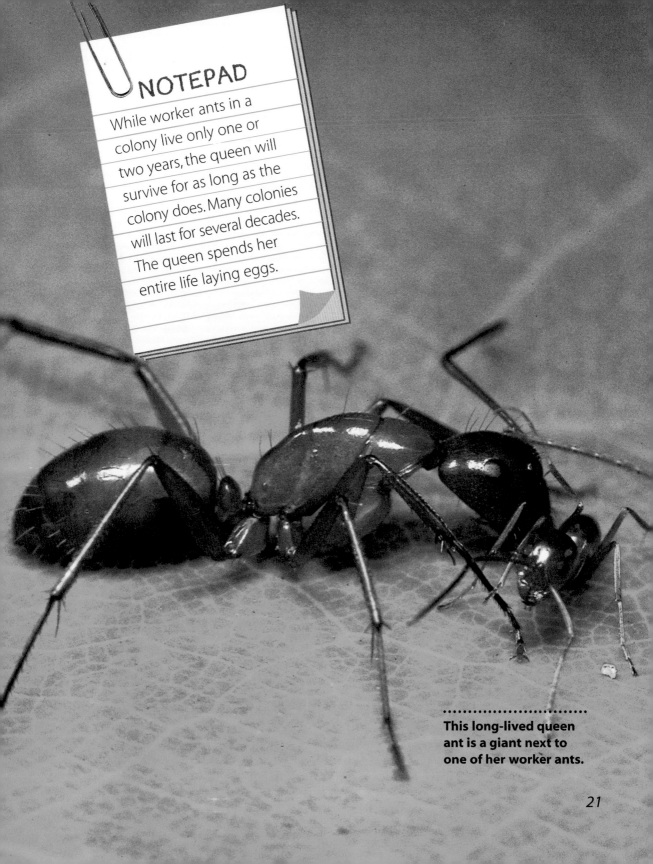

NOTEPAD

While worker ants in a colony live only one or two years, the queen will survive for as long as the colony does. Many colonies will last for several decades. The queen spends her entire life laying eggs.

This long-lived queen ant is a giant next to one of her worker ants.

21

Locust

What's the insect that TRAVELS FARTHEST in migration?

The Desert Locust

Certain kinds of locusts have been known to travel nearly 3,000 miles (4,500 kilometers). One species flew from Africa across the Atlantic Ocean to South America!

The desert locust is the insect traveling champion.

NOTEPAD

This locust is honored with another incredible insect distinction: it holds the record for the largest swarms. In Africa in 1954, a swarm of desert locusts invaded Kenya and covered an area of 77 square miles (200 square kilometers).

Scientists estimate that there were more than 50 million locusts per 1 square kilometer, making a total number of 10 billion locusts in one swarm!

What's the insect with the FASTEST WING BEAT?

The Midge

This tiny, fly-like creature can beat its wings at a frequency of 1046 hertz— that means more than 1,000 times per second! By comparison, a common housefly beats its wings only about 180 times per second.

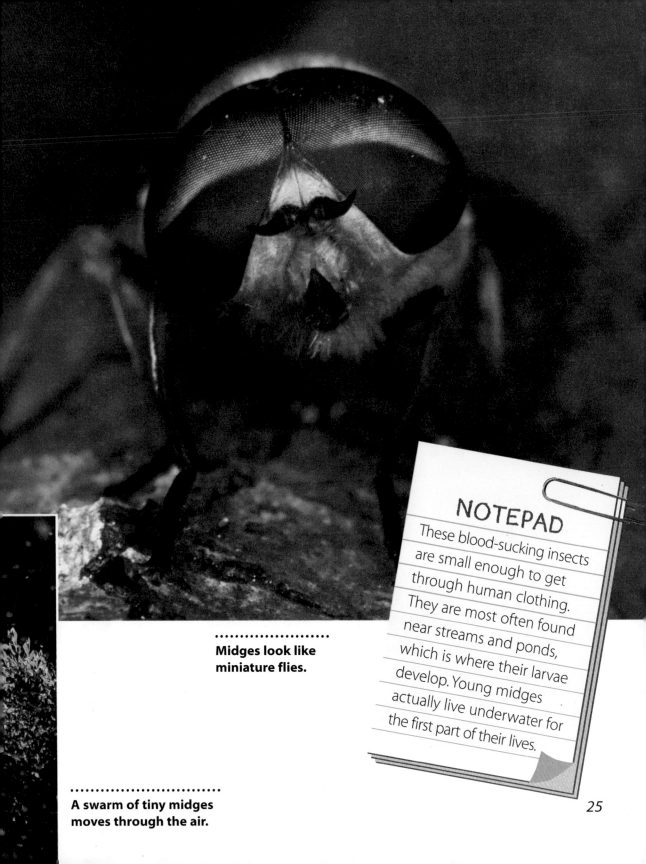

Midges look like
miniature flies.

NOTEPAD

These blood-sucking insects are small enough to get through human clothing. They are most often found near streams and ponds, which is where their larvae develop. Young midges actually live underwater for the first part of their lives.

A swarm of tiny midges
moves through the air.

Scavenger ants are some of the few animals that can survive the harsh environment of the Sahara Desert.

What's the insect that can withstand the MOST HEAT?

The Scavenger Ant

Desert-dwelling scavenger ants can be found in the Sahara Desert of Africa, as well as in North American deserts in the southwest. Some species have been known to go out hunting in temperatures above 140 degrees Fahrenheit (60 degrees C)!

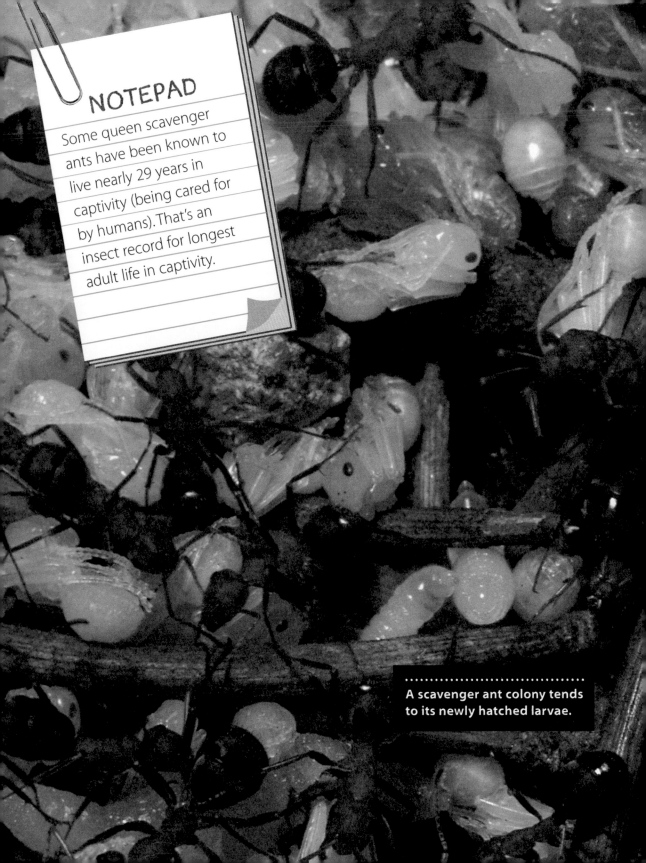

A scavenger ant colony tends to its newly hatched larvae.

What's the insect that gives off the BRIGHTEST LIGHT?

The Jamaican Click Beetle

The light flashes of this very large beetle species have been recorded as the brightest of all insects. By comparison, the click beetle's light is thought to be about 10 times brighter than that of a common firefly (which is not really a fly— it's another kind of beetle).

28

Click beetle

The Jamaican click beetle is also called the eyed click beetle.

NOTEPAD
The ability of an insect to glow or give off light is called bioluminescence (bi•oh•loo•mih•neh•sense). Certain insects have developed this ability in order to flash messages in the dark to possible mates.

Atlas moth
caterpillar

What's the insect with the LARGEST WINGS?

The Atlas Moth

In terms of overall wing surface area, this huge Asian moth holds the record. With wings that can extend more than 9 or 10 inches (23–25 centimeters), some atlas moths have a wing surface area of roughly 16 to 17 square inches (12 square centimeters) per wing!

The atlas moth—shown nearly actual size—is a giant in the world of flying insects.

Glossary

Behemoth—something of monstrous size and power.

Bioluminescence—the emission of light from living organisms.

Colony—a large group of insects that live and work together.

Decibel—unit for measuring the volume of sounds.

Hertz—unit for measuring the frequency of vibrations and waves, equal to one cycle per second.

Host—an animal or plant from which a parasite gets nutrition.

Larva—an insect in the stage of development between egg and adult, when it looks like a worm.

Migration—when animals or insects go to live in another region or climate at a certain time of the year or point in their lives.

Molt—to shed an outer covering so a new one can grow.

Protein—a nourishing substance found in all plant and animal cells.

Species—one of the groups into which animals are divided according to their shared characteristics.

Thorax—the part of an insect's body between its head and its abdomen.

Venom—poison produced by some insects.

For More Information

Books

Anderson, Margaret Jean. *Bizarre Insects.* Springfield, NJ: Enslow Publishers, Inc., 1996.
Parker, Steve. Ann Salvage (Illustrator). *Beastly Bugs* (Creepy Creatures). Chatham, NY: Raintree Steck Vaughn, 1993.
Wechsler, Doug. *Bizarre Bugs.* New York, NY: Cobblehill, 1995.

Videos

James Earl Jones. *Insects: The Little Things That Run the World* (1989).

Web Sites

Fun Insect Facts
Uncover strange facts about well-known insects—ham.spu.umn.edu/kris/science.html.

Get This Bug Off Me!
Broaden your understanding of the insect world by learning which bugs are dangerous and which are harmless—www.uky.edu/Agriculture/Entomology/ythfacts/hurtrnot.htm.

Index